PROJECT MANAGEMENT HANDBOOK

Simplified Agile, Scrum and DevOps for Beginners

Written by:
Jack C. Stanley and Erik D. Gross
Co-Founders of The Tech Academy

TABLE OF CONTENTS

TABLE OF CONTENTS

TABLE OF CONTENTS

Chapter	Title	Page number

INTRODUCTION

We wrote this book to provide an easy, "one-stop shop" for project management.

As the cover states, this book includes the basics of:

1. Project management – the art of completing tasks through running people and organizing.

2. Agile – a type of project management that focuses on teamwork and flexibility.

3. Scrum – the most popular form of Agile, named after the rugby term "Scrum" (packing players close together in an attempt to gain possession of a ball).

4. DevOps – short for Development and Operations; a business practice that coordinates the work of technology professionals with the work of employees not typically involved in technology projects, in an attempt to increase collaboration, improve efficiency and speed up project completion.

Each of these subjects will be explained in this book.

We found that there weren't any manuals that describe these topics in one location, so we compiled the information to offer a handbook that can be used by technical and non-technical people alike.

CHAPTER 1:
WHAT IS SOFTWARE DEVELOPMENT?

This book covers project management as it relates to software development. Even given that focus, most of the information will be beneficial to any industry.

Software development refers to the creation of computer programs and websites. Computer programs are sets of instructions executed (performed) by computers for a particular purpose or sets of purposes. Programs are also referred to as "applications" or "software".

Software development is also called "coding", "computer programming" and "software engineering". Each of these terms mean basically the same thing: to tell computers what to do using code.

Code is the words and symbols used to communicate instructions to a computer. Code is written in various programming languages. Programming languages are organized systems of words, phrases and symbols that let you create programs. There are many different types of programming languages, each of which was created to fill a specific purpose. For example, some languages are better suited for creating computer games, while others are better used for making phone apps.

It is not necessary to know how to code to read this book. We wrote this book assuming no technical background or experience on the part of the reader – anyone can pick up this book and learn about these fundamental concepts.

So, what is project management?

CHAPTER 2:
WHAT IS PROJECT MANAGEMENT?

A "project" is something taken on with some sort of an end goal in mind. It comes from the Latin word *proiectum*, which means "projection".

"Management" means to organize, coordinate and control something effectively. It comes from the Latin word *maneggiare*, which meant "to handle; shape".

In the technology industry, "project management" is the practice of starting, planning, controlling and completing the work on a coding project. Typically, project management relates to coordinating the actions of an entire team – from the client the project is being done for, to the developers, to the people checking the quality of the work done on the project.

The "client" is the customer. This is the person or company that work is being done for. Typically, the client has paid a fee in exchange for the work. When dealing with clients, it is recommended that you deliver exactly what the client asks for, as opposed to a version that differs from their vision.

The "developers" are the creators of software. They are the ones who write the code that builds the software.

Project management includes formulating plans, assigning roles, acquiring appropriate tools and materials, developing and managing schedules, conveying information, promoting good communication, meeting milestones (significant stages in development), and exhibiting strong leadership skills to ultimately resolve and complete the project within the agreed-upon deadline.

In fact, the purpose of project management is to ensure that projects are accurately completed on or ahead of schedule.

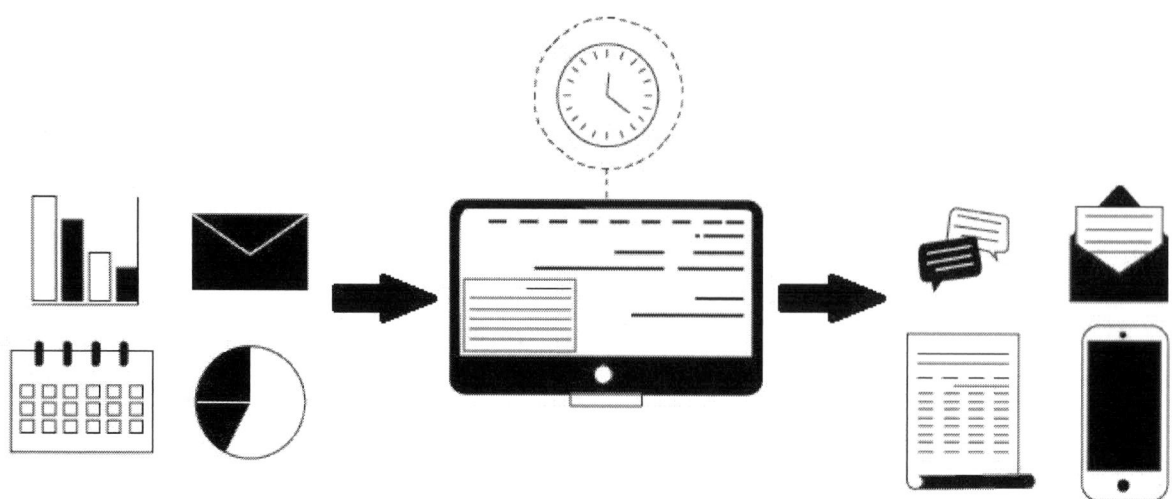

Project management has existed for as long as humankind. It was used over 2,300 years ago in the building of the Great Wall of China, it is used today, and it will continue to be used. It is the science of utilizing people to execute plans.

This book will cover the most popular types of project management in use today.

Let's go over who it is that oversees project management in a company.

CHAPTER 3:
PROJECT MANAGER

The project manager is responsible for leading a project from the beginning to the end. This includes the planning of a project, execution of a project, delivering the project on time (on a schedule and on a budget), as well as managing the people and resources.

They pull this off by ensuring regular deliverables. Deliverables are measurable things that are brought about as the result of work. A deliverable is a "done" – something that has been completed. They're quantifiable goods or services that are produced.

Project managers work with the team to ensure that the desired outcome is achieved and that work is completed in the correct sequence.

Project managers commonly coordinate with clients, direct the overall plan, define the scope of the project, set milestones, monitor progress, evaluate performance and attempt to complete projects on or ahead of schedule and on or under budget.

Here are some of the other duties of the project manager:

- Leading and managing the team.

- Figuring out the project schedule.

- Assigning tasks to other team members.

- Providing regular updates to upper management.

The project manager is the person who runs a project team – let's look at what that is.

CHAPTER 4:
PROJECT TEAMS

The project team is the people involved in working together on a project to achieve its goals.

Project teams are composed of the project manager, all project management staff, the software development team, and anyone else involved in work related to the project.

The project manager is the boss over the project team and is ultimately responsible for the success and quality of the project.

Project team members have a wide range of duties and responsibilities – again, they are anyone other than the project manager who is involved in the project. This includes employees and even outside consultants. The typical duties of project team members include:

- Contributing to the project's objectives.

- Completing individual assigned tasks.

- Providing advice and feedback.

- Working with users (the people that use the software) to determine their needs.

- Documenting all work done.

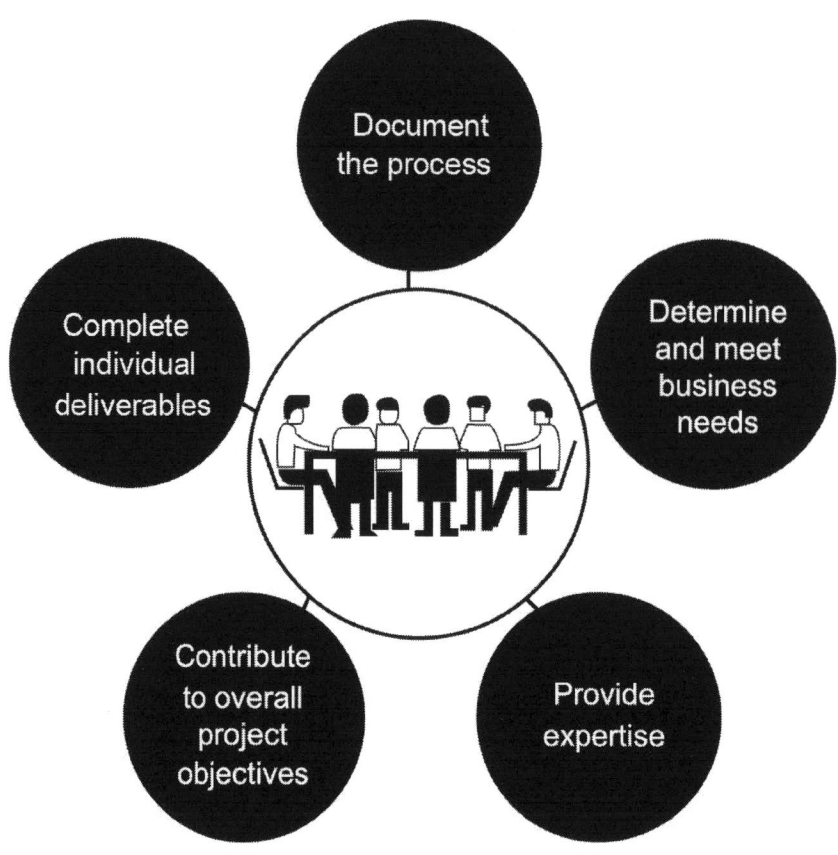

What section of a company is responsible for its project management policies and procedures?

CHAPTER 5:
PROJECT MANAGEMENT OFFICE

The project management office (abbreviated PMO) is a team or department inside a company that oversees all project management. Specifically, they define and maintain the standards for project management.

The project management office creates the needed documentation, provides guidance and determines how to measure success. They are the office responsible for a business's project management policies.

Let's take a look at a common sequence used in project management to create software.

CHAPTER 6:
PROJECT MANAGEMENT LIFE CYCLE

"Life cycle" literally refers to the stages of one's life – from birth to death.

The project management life cycle is the various phases that software development goes through, including:

1. Initiation (start).

2. Planning.

3. Execution.

4. Monitoring.

5. Closure (completion).

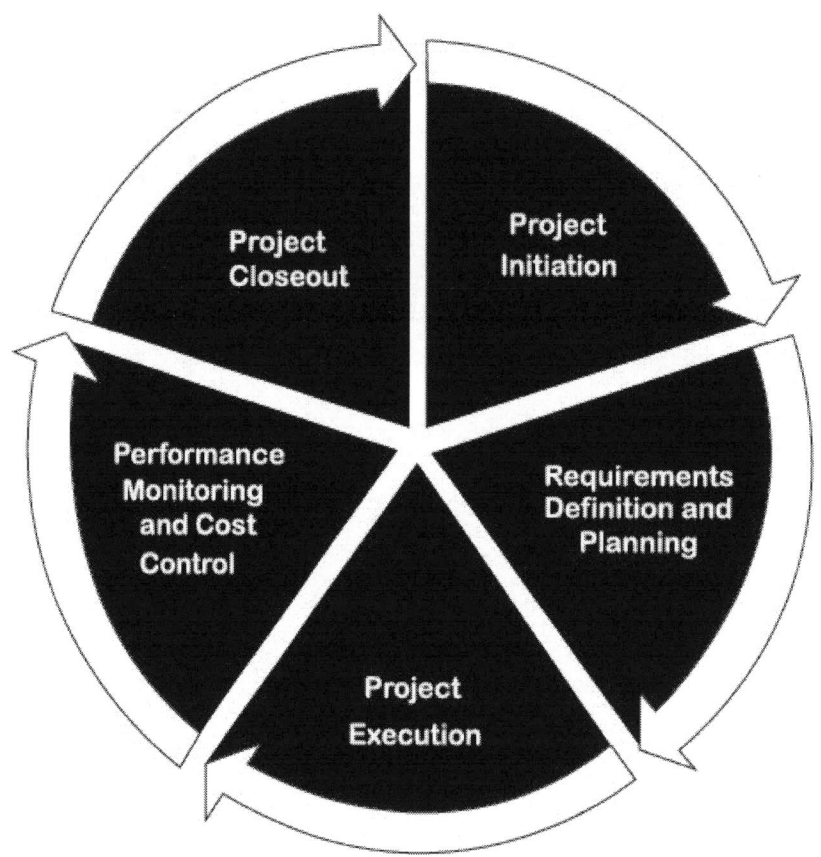

The project management life cycle includes:

- Keeping documentation.

- Working to meet deadlines.

- Obtaining compliance.

- Reducing overall production time.

- Maintaining support.

- Improving product quality and reliability.

- Avoiding expensive issues through improved forecasting (future prediction).

- Lessening production costs.

The project management life cycle is considered linear (in a line; sequenced) project management. There are nonlinear (not in a fixed sequence; fluid) project management techniques as well, which we will cover later in this book.

Linear project management styles are referred to as waterfall project management. So, what is that?

CHAPTER 7:
WATERFALL PROJECT MANAGEMENT

Waterfall is an approach to project management where work is completed in distinct stages. Each stage is moved through, step by step, eventually resulting in the release of the product to its users. It is a linear approach to project management.

An important element of linear project management (waterfall) is that the plan is first made in full and then adhered to throughout the entire project. It is a firm and rigid approach to project management and doesn't easily allow for changes throughout the process.

Deploy means to spread something out or arrange it in a strategic fashion. In coding, deploy means to ensure software (or hardware) is fully set up and running properly. This includes installation, testing, making necessary changes and more.

A release is deployable software. It is the distribution of a working version of an application. The product is being "released" to its users.

In the waterfall picture below, each step would be completed before moving on to the next step:

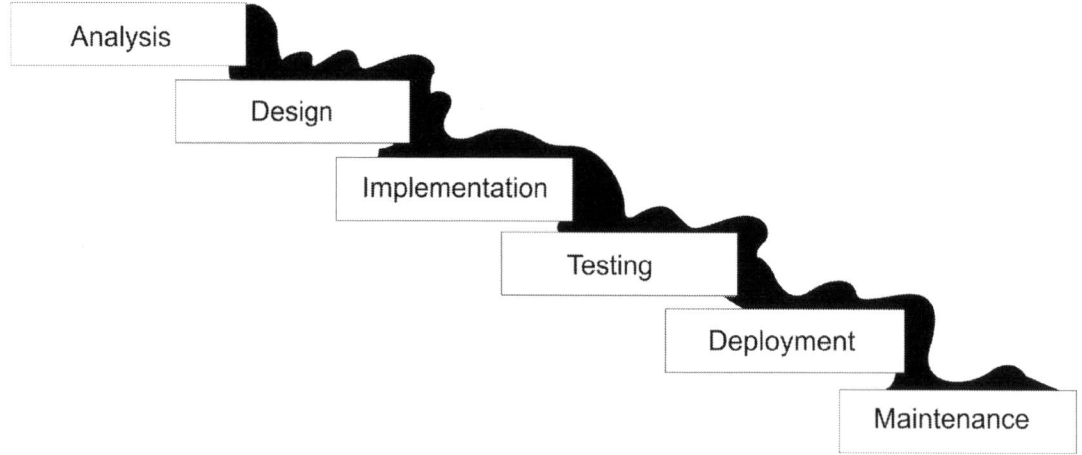

Now, let's dive into some popular project management terms.

CHAPTER 8:
EXECUTIVE SUMMARIES

An executive summary (also called a management summary) is a short document that is created for various business purposes. Executive summaries can be used to outline longer reports or to summarize large proposals.

The purpose of executive summaries is to provide brief overviews that allow readers to become familiar with the overall data much more rapidly (as opposed to reading longer reports in full).

The origin of the term comes from the fact that teams were provided with summaries by executives for rapid decision making and project approvals. Executive summaries are still commonly used for this purpose.

Executive summaries are sometimes used in project management to provide snapshots of various projects and proposals.

Let's take a look at how to convey the purpose of a project.

CHAPTER 9:
BUSINESS CASES

A business case is a description of the reasons for starting a project or tasks. The "why" for a particular project is its business case.

Business cases should include the specific business need behind the project and the benefits that it brings. They can be written or conveyed verbally. In addition to the reasons why and the benefits, business cases can include:

- The various options associated with the project.

- The cost of the project.

- The expected risks connected to the project.

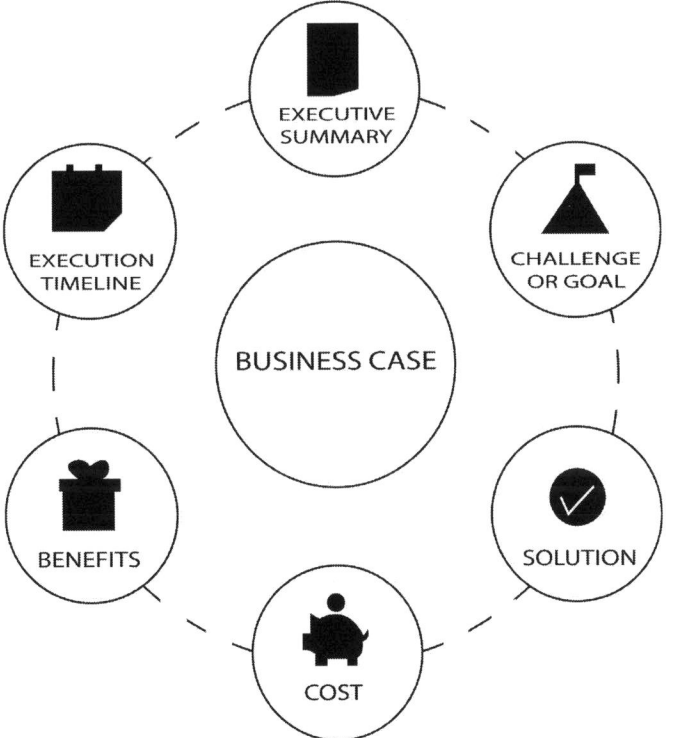

Another element of business cases can be a "gap analysis". A gap analysis is a comparison between current performance and the potential or desired performance.

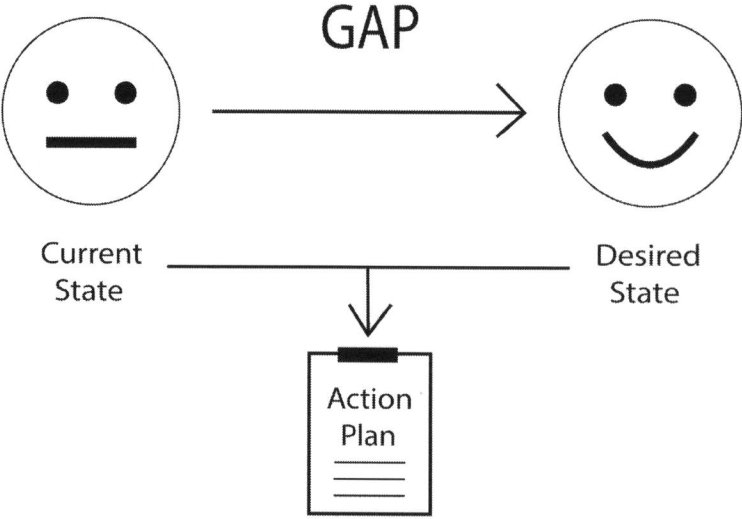

To summarize, a thorough business case for a project includes: the reasons behind it, associated risks, benefits, various options or approaches, an executive summary, and a gap analysis.

Sometimes when writing code, there are better ways of doing certain things. Let's cover the word for that.

CHAPTER 10:
REFACTORING CODE

Refactor means to rewrite code with the purpose of improving its structure and readability, without changing its behavior.

Streamlining your code, cleaning it up, or making it more concise could all be considered refactoring.

Let's say you created a script (a program that automates something) that scanned websites for company phone numbers. Your program is made up of 250 lines of code. You go through your code and you're able to decrease your total lines of code to 100, while still maintaining the initial purpose of your script, and possibly getting it to perform faster – that would be refactoring.

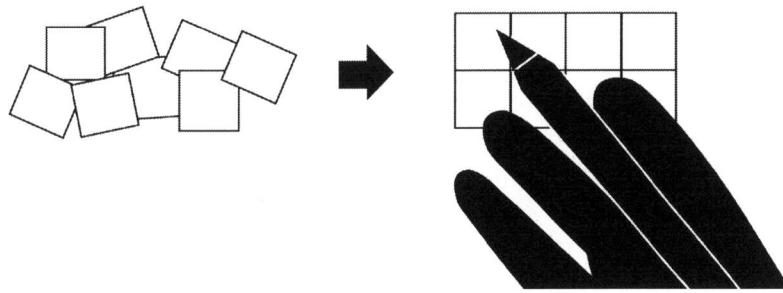

"Production code" refers to live code that users interact with. For example, the Facebook app you see on your phone is production code. This is as opposed to code that is being tested or hasn't been deployed yet. Typically, refactoring occurs with production code. Meaning, the code is refactored and re-released in better form.

One of the common elements of software development is testing. So, let's discuss that.

CHAPTER 11:
TESTING

Quality assurance (abbreviated QA) simply refers to ensuring that standards are maintained – it is literally actions taken to assure quality. In coding, it means the same thing. QA are actions that make sure that software performs as expected.

The main component of QA is testing. Testing software is the process of putting the software through various tests to attempt to locate bugs that need to be fixed.

A bug is an error in a computer program that impairs or prevents its operation. A bug could slow something down on your computer or stop it altogether. Some say this term came from incidents during the early days of computers where actual bugs (insects) got inside the computer and caused malfunctions.

QA and testing are intrinsic elements of project management.

There's actually software that can automate the process of testing. This QA software can test some of the software for you and provide you with detailed reports on potential issues.

Acceptance testing is a form of quality assurance that tests software to see if it complies with the project requirements. The purpose is to determine whether or not the product is ready for delivery (completion).

Unit testing is a way to test software where individual units (individual parts) of code are tested as opposed to the entire software all at once. These units of code are categorized by setting related sections of the computer program together and running them through various tests.

A unit test is a short program that checks the results of and tests various units of code.

They are valuable because they can detect when refactoring code has resulted in the code not working as originally designed.

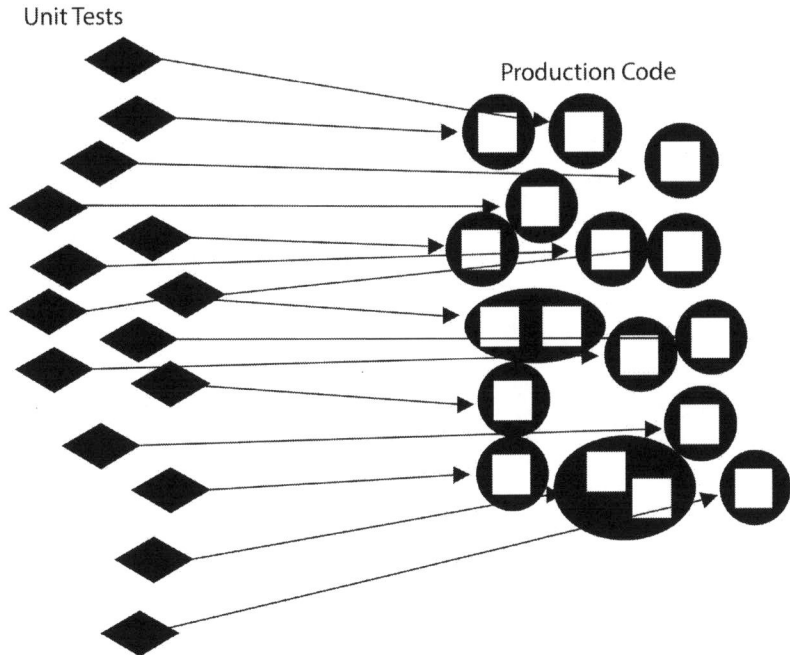

Another form of testing is usability testing. This tests how easily software can be utilized by users.

Here are some of the points evaluated in usability testing:

- What is the level of skill required to learn and use the software?

- How long does it take to begin using the software?

- What is the user's attitude toward the software?

- How does the user respond to the software under realistic conditions?

Usability testing can be used for these reasons:

Uncover Problems
in the design

Discover Opportunities
to improve the design

Learn About Users
behavior and preferences

The purpose of QA and testing is to ensure that the project is a success. So, how do you gauge the potential success of a project?

CHAPTER 12:
FEASIBILITY STUDY

"Feasible" means "workable; realistic; possible".

A feasibility study is a review of how practical a proposed project is. The purpose is to analyze the strengths and weaknesses of a project. This includes confronting the various opportunities and threats, the required resources, and how likely success is.

The primary points that are reviewed in feasibility testing are:

1. The required cost of the project, and

2. The value attained by completing the project.

Feasibility studies can provide a historical background of the company or project, a description of the proposed project or service, financial information, details about various activities, market research, and legal requirements.

Feasibility tests are supposed to be unbiased and provide a realistic view of the potential of success.

A project includes a project manager, project team, clients and more. What do we call all of these people?

CHAPTER 13:
STAKEHOLDERS

A stakeholder is someone involved in a project that is concerned with its overall success.

The origin of the word is "a person involved in a bet".

In project management, a stakeholder is simply anyone interested in a project's outcome. This can include members of the team, executives, users and clients.

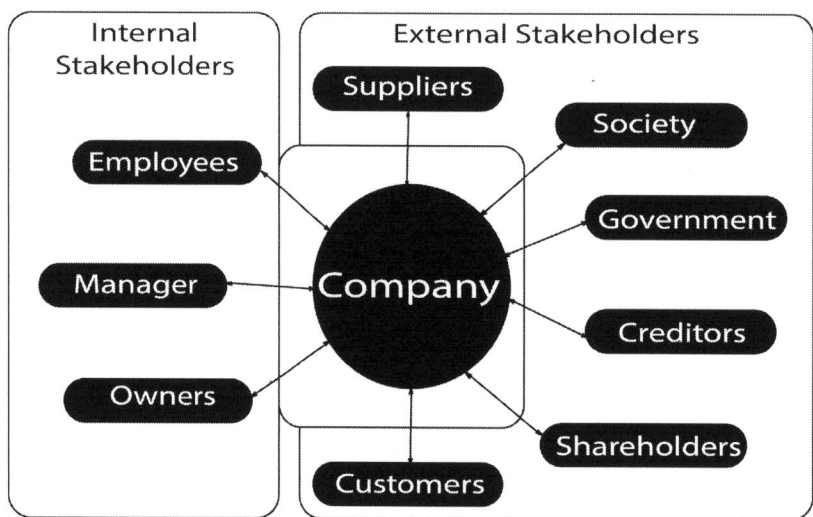

Stakeholders are the people affected by the outcome of a project and those who can influence it.

Now let's go over what is considered to be the first product aimed for in project management.

CHAPTER 14:
MVPs

Viable literally means "able to survive" and refers to something that can operate successfully.

A Minimum Viable Product (abbreviated MVP) is a version of a product with just enough features to satisfy early customers and provide feedback for future product development.

It is not a completed project but can be used to show basic functions.

For example, an MVP app may be able to produce some basic actions but might not look aesthetically pleasing yet.

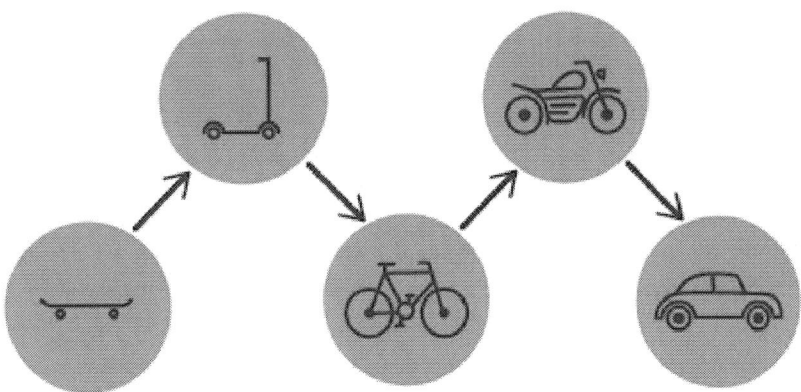

Now, how are the sizes and goals of a project established?

CHAPTER 15:
PROJECT CHARTERS

A "charter" is a written description of something – such as an explanation of a company's functions.

A project charter is a statement about the scope (size and range), goals and participants (people involved) in a project. It is written before the work begins on a project and covers the following:

1. A description of various positions and their associated responsibilities.

2. Outlines of the main goals of the project.

3. Identifies the primary stakeholders.

4. Defines the role, duties and responsibilities of the project manager.

Project charters can be used to gain authorization on a project or provide a point of focus for the project that can be referred back to later.

Let's cover what the term is for the beginning-to-end of a project.

CHAPTER 16:
LEAD TIME

Lead time is how much time has passed since the client initially ordered the project and the completion of the project. It is the amount of time between project requirements and their fulfillment.

Here's how lead time could apply to ordering food at a restaurant:

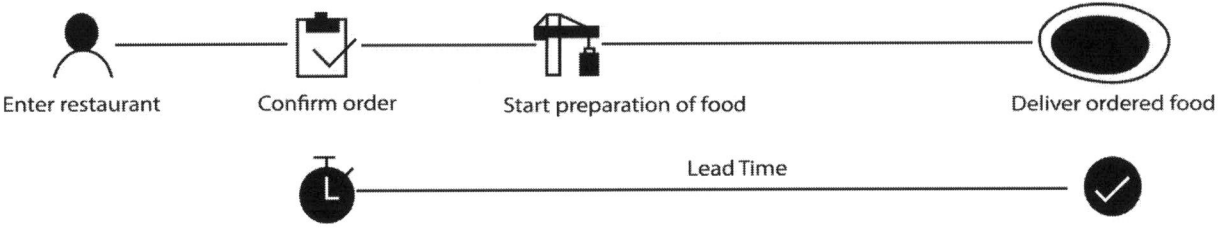

Lead time is used in another related way in project management. It applies when you have two tasks that have a dependency – that is, one task requires some or all of the work involved in the other task to be completed before it can be started.

In this use, lead time means "the amount of time between the start of one activity and the start of a second activity dependent on the first".

A project manager might use this idea in setting a time schedule for various tasks to be completed – for example, they might need to push the launch date of a new web site two weeks out into the future because that is how long it will take for the shipping, arrival and setup of the computer that the web site will be installed on. Here, the "lead time" of the web site installation is two weeks, since we have to wait that long before we can start that task.

Now that we understand some of the terms associated with project management, let's circle back to the project management life cycle to take a deeper look into each stage.

CHAPTER 17:
INITIATION

The first stage in the project management life cycle is the initiation or conception stage.

The initiation phase can include:

- Meeting with the client to nail down their needs and wants.

- Creating a business case (reasons for project, its benefits, risks, etc.).

- Performing a feasibility study (required cost and potential value).

- Establishing a project charter (description of roles, responsibilities and goals).

- Assigning your project team (including the project manager).

- Setting up the project office (staff that oversee project management policies).

Now let's go over the next step!

CHAPTER 18:
PLANNING

The second phase in the project management lifecycle is the planning phase – also called the design phase. During the planning phase, the client is involved for a deeper dive into exact project specifications.

As the name states, the planning phase includes developing a plan for the project, including the project timeline, tasks to be performed, and identifying possible constraints.

A constraint is a limitation or restriction. In project management, a constraint is anything that can delay or cause issues for a project, such as:

- Time

- Cost

- Size

- Quality

- Risks

The planning phase additionally includes these steps:

1. Completing the financial planning and budgets – estimating cost.

2. Gathering all needed resources – including putting together the team.

In this phase, we finalize the plans that we began in the initiation phase. This is where the final client approval on the project plan is obtained from the client.

After the plan is fully figured out, a project kickoff meeting is held where the project team is gathered and brought up to speed on everything.

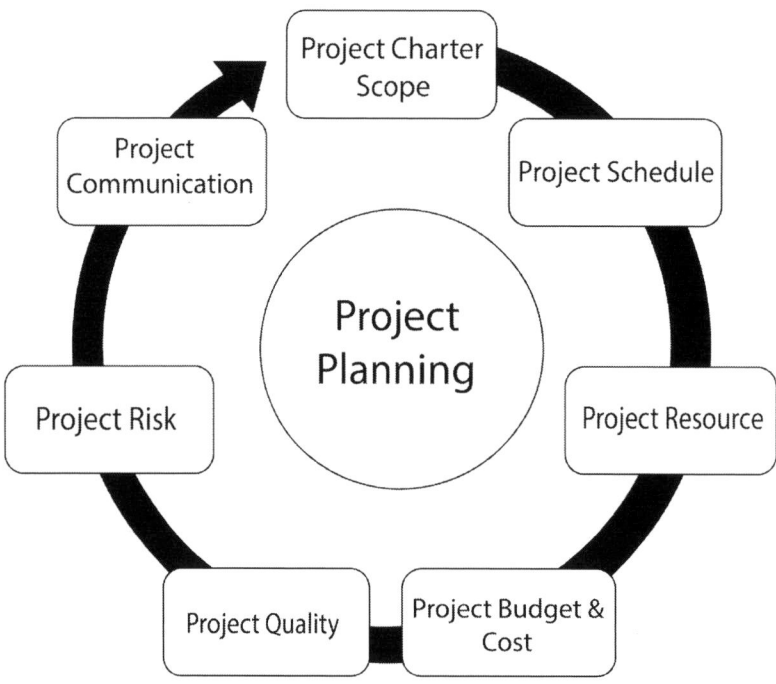

After phase two, we move into phase three.

CHAPTER 19:
EXECUTION

In the third phase of the project management lifecycle, execution, we get to work!

This is where all the preceding planning, analysis and research is put to use.

The execution phase includes:

- Software development – actual coding.

- Holding regular meetings to assign tasks, check in on projects and debug.

- Communicating with clients and management.

Then we move into the fourth phase.

CHAPTER 20:
MONITORING

The fourth phase of the project management life cycle is monitoring. Technically, some of this occurs concurrently to phase 3 and some people actually consider them to be the same phase.

The monitoring phase consists of ensuring that quality is maintained. This stage consists of:

- Determining if a project is on schedule and on budget.

- Monitoring changes that occur with planning and the project – taking into account various issues that arise and how to handle them.

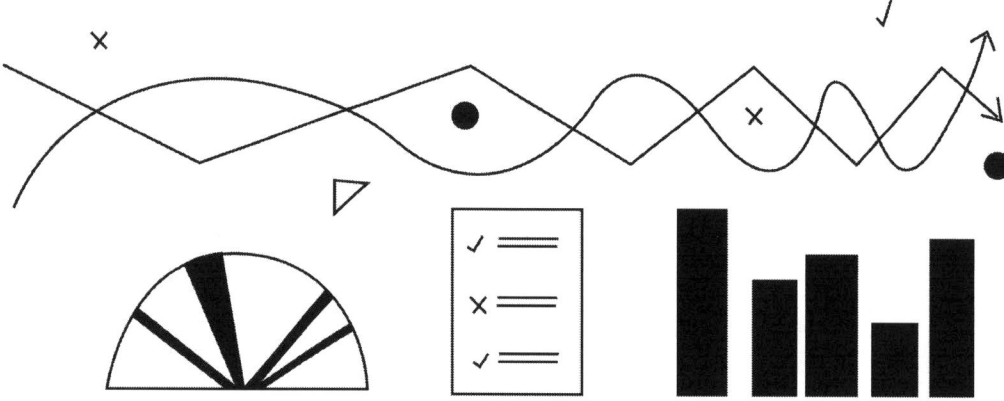

Phases three and four end with the deployment and delivery of the finished product.

Then we move to the last stage of the process.

CHAPTER 21:
CLOSURE

The last step in the project management life cycle is the completion – also referred to as the closure phase.

This occurs after the product is passed over to the client. This phase might include continued product support, documentation and maintenance.

This final phase includes:

- Analyzing the performance of the project and determining whether or not the project's goals were met. This could include questions like:
  - "Were all the tasks completed?"
  - "Was the project completed on time?"
  - "Did we stay on budget?"

- Reviewing the performance of the team and evaluating how each person performed. This includes determining who finished their assigned tasks and the level of quality produced by each member.

- Completing all documentation and wrapping up all loose ends.

- Holding retrospective (looking back on something) meetings to see what lessons were learned. The purpose of this is to implement this data in future projects.

Basically, the project is finalized in this phase.

Now, we've talked about the waterfall approach. What's the opposite of that?

CHAPTER 22:
ADAPTING

Adaptive planning refers to changing one's approach mid-production. A static (unchanging) plan would be a plan that is made and adhered to from beginning to end.

With adaptive planning, adjustments are made throughout the work process based on new data and unforeseen occurrences.

In software development, evolutionary development is an iterative (repeating a sequence wherein each step in the sequence brings one closer to the end goal) and incremental (done in small stages) approach.

This approach breaks tasks down into "bite-sized" chunks and progresses projects forward in small steps.

This is as opposed to knocking out the whole project in one big push.

You now have a basic understanding of project management – well done!

Now let's discuss one of the most popular project management methodologies in the tech industry.

CHAPTER 23:
AGILE

Agile literally means "able to move quickly and easily". In project management, Agile is a methodology that is popular in the computer industry.

A "methodology" is simply a way to do something. It is the methods, techniques and approach to getting something done. There are several different project management methodologies, and Agile is one of the most-used.

Agile is best understood in terms of how it differs from more traditional methods for project management.

As we've covered, traditional project management is characterized by a linear (step-by-step; sequential) approach that usually has some or all of these broad steps:

1. Initiation (starting the project).
2. Planning.
3. Execution.
4. Monitoring.
5. Completion.

Agile project management methodology, first introduced in the late 1980s, is characterized by a non-linear approach. Instead of being completed in the "Planning" step, requirements and solutions evolve throughout the process through collaboration between self-organizing, cross-functional teams.

Execution of project work is done continuously throughout the life of the project. Agile methods involve adaptive planning, evolutionary development, early delivery, and continuous improvement. Agile encourages rapid and flexible response to change.

This method is increasingly popular and is often used to manage the process of creating software. It focuses on teamwork and finishing one feature of the software at a time (fully) before moving onto the next.

We covered some of the primary data and terms related to project management. Now let's look at some concepts and words that apply to Agile.

In summary, Agile is a method of project management that focuses on dividing tasks into short phases of work, with frequent reviews of the project and adaption of planning mid-execution as needed. An Agile approach is flexible and less rigid than some other methods of project management.

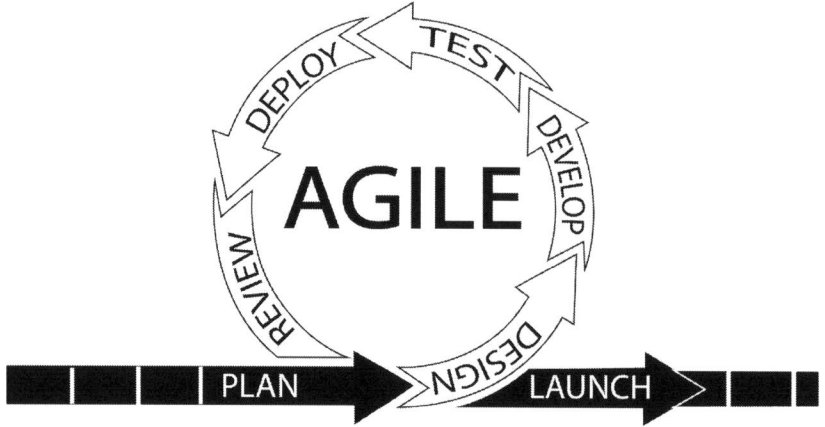

One of the characteristics of Agile is that it's incremental. Let's go over what that means.

CHAPTER 24:
INCREMENTAL DEVELOPMENT

An increment is a small step. Incremental refers to moving forward in stages.

Incremental development is a practice where software is designed, deployed and tested incrementally (a little bit more added each time) until the project is completed. Each step builds on the previous with additional advancements.

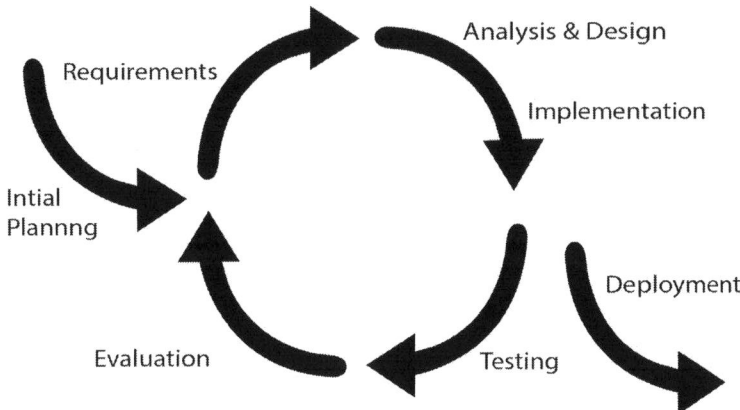

Another characteristic of Agile is that it is iterative. Let's go over what that means!

CHAPTER 25:
ITERATIVE DEVELOPMENT

Iterative means performing repeatedly.

Iterative development refers to developing software through repeated cycles (iterations). These cycles each accomplish some sort of a minimum viable product. For example:

First iteration: Create a basic homepage.

Second iteration: Add the ability for a user to create an account and log in.

Third iteration: Add the ability to change your password.

Fourth iteration: Add a page that displays account information.

Etc.

One of the actions included in Agile is a regular meeting called the daily standup. Let's look at what this is.

CHAPTER 26:
DAILY STANDUPS

Daily standups are a daily meeting involving certain employees who are working on a project. It is meant to last 5-15 minutes. Often the attendees actually stand up. This is meant to encourage participants to keep the meeting short.

Each person tells the group the answers to these three questions:

1. What did I accomplish yesterday?

2. What will I do today?

3. What obstacles are impeding my progress?

Daily standups help ensure that obstacles to getting your work done are identified and handled rapidly.

The whole purpose of project management is to *complete tasks*. Let's go over how these are tracked in Agile.

CHAPTER 27:
PRODUCT BACKLOGS

You may have heard the word "backlog" used to refer to work that is overdue or should have been done already. For example, if you didn't answer your emails for a month, you would have a backlog of emails.

In Agile, a backlog is slightly different. It simply means: work needing to be done. Any work that is supposed to happen is considered a backlog. Often it refers to upcoming work that has not yet been assigned to a worker or a target completion date.

For example, if you were making a software program that would allow you to manage the members, vehicles and schedules for a car club, you would break down what you had to do in order to implement those functions into many individual tasks. That list is your backlog. As you completed items, they would be removed from the backlog.

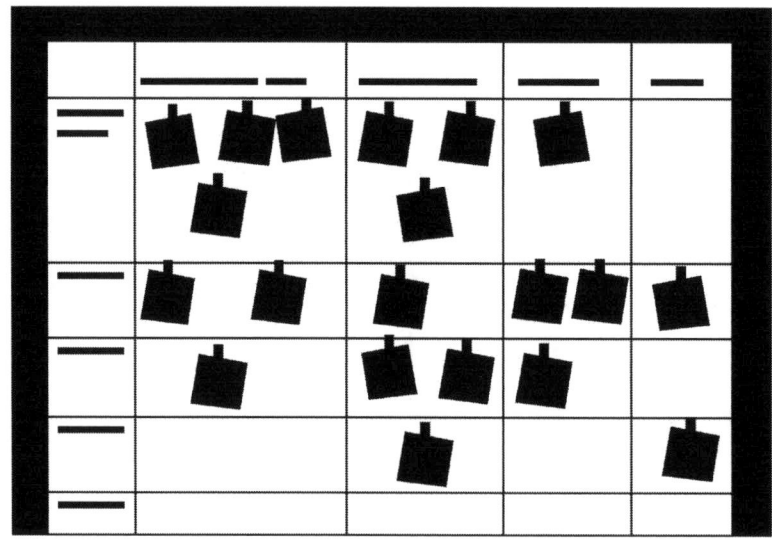

Now let's cover how Agile manages time.

CHAPTER 28:
SPRINTS

A sprint is a set period of time (usually 1 week, 2 weeks or 30 days) where a specified amount of work is assigned to get done.

Sprints begin and end with meetings where tasks are assigned and reviews of past performance are done.

Agile breaks up projects into sprints. During each day of a sprint, daily standups occur where the progress of the project is covered.

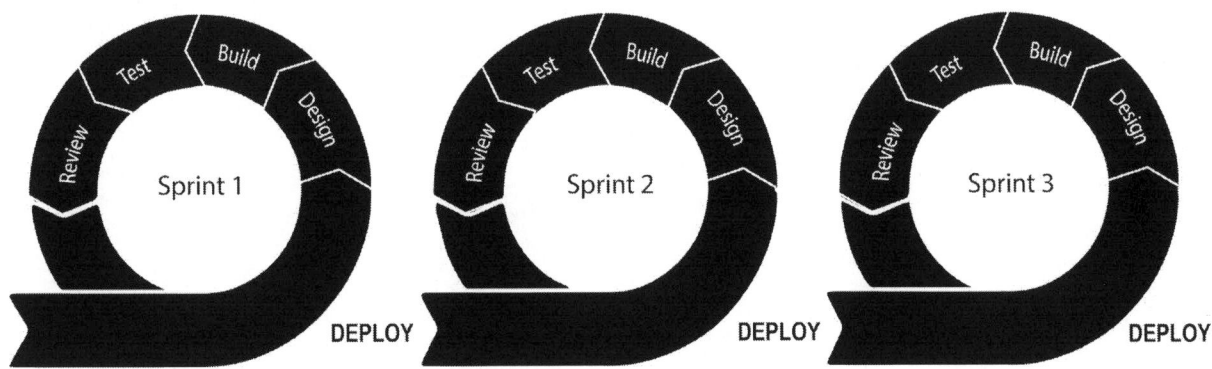

The sprint goal is the key focus and overall product of a particular sprint. It is also referred to as the theme.

Now that you have a basic understanding of Agile project management, let's take a look at the most popular branch (sub-category) of Agile.

CHAPTER 29:
SCRUM

Scrum is one of the implementations of Agile.

The term "scrum" comes from a rugby term that consists of teammates interlocking their arms and pushing forward into opponents.

In the technology world, Scrum is a method of project management that consists of tightly coordinated teamwork, strong organization and completing projects according to client demands. Most software development projects use Scrum nowadays. There are a set of terms and techniques that are used in Scrum but it all centers around teamwork.

Whereas Agile is a methodology, Scrum is a framework. This is only mentioned here so that you know there is technically a difference between the two terms.

A methodology is a set of rules, methods and tools that can be used to achieve a particular goal. A framework is an overview of how guidelines should be implemented. Frameworks are typically considered a "looser" and more flexible structure that allows for other tools to be included. Methodologies are considered more rigid, while frameworks allow more leeway.

Even though frameworks are usually considered to be less strict than methodologies, Scrum has evolved to a point where it has very precise procedures. There are even certifications that can be obtained. In reality, it is expected that both Agile and Scrum are applied as outlined in this book.

All of the Agile terms and concepts covered in this book so far are used in Scrum, including:

- Sprints (fixed amount of times of work, such as 1 week, 2 weeks, etc.).

- Backlogs (list of work needing to be done).

- Standups (daily meetings of the development team)

In Scrum, these terms are either used as listed above or sometimes referred to with the word "Scrum" added – like Scrum Sprints or Daily Scrum Meeting. Again, they mean the same thing as in Agile because Scrum is Agile.

One way to look at Scrum's relationship to Agile is this picture:

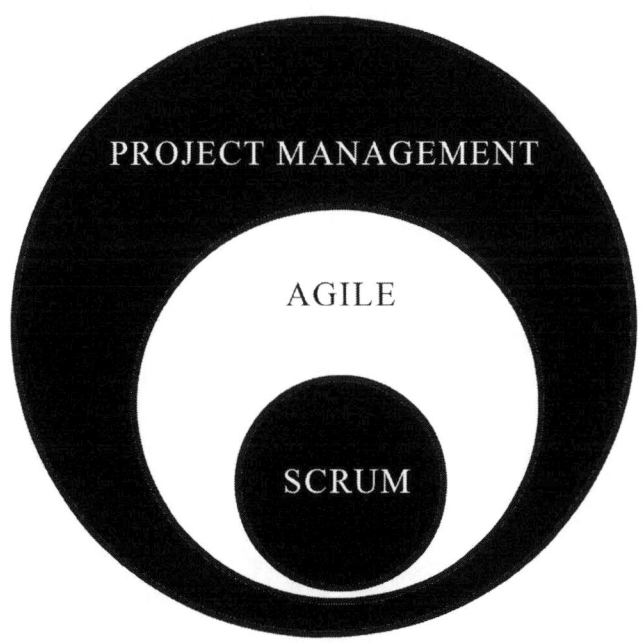

Or to look at it another way:

In this example, "sports" is project management, "basketball" is Agile and "NBA" (the most popular application of basketball) is Scrum.

Now that you know what Scrum is, let's go over some more Scrum-related words and topics.

CHAPTER 30:
PRODUCT OWNER

In Agile and Scrum, the Product Owner is the person who has final authority in representing the customer's interests.

The Product Owner is available to the project's team at any time (even though they are not involved in the actual creation of the project) and is present at most meetings. They are the "boss" of the project but they allow the members to set their own targets and manage themselves.

The Product Owner is typically the person who meets regularly with the client.

Some of their duties include:

- Clearly expressing backlog tasks

- Ensuring that the backlog is visible and clear to everyone

- Ensuring that everyone knows what the priorities are and what to work on next

As these duties show, the Product Owner is ultimately responsible for the product backlog.

The word "owner" refers to responsibility – the Product Owner *owns* that the product will be accurately developed.

The Product Owner views projects from the client's perspective and works to ensure that their vision is accomplished.

There is another person involved in running the day-to-day activities of Scrum.

CHAPTER 31:
SCRUM MASTER

The Scrum Master is the person actually involved in the computer programming/software development, who coordinates the group activities and runs them. The Scrum Master is there, on the ground, performing work and helping their fellow teammates. The same person need not be the Scrum Master over a long period of time; some teams have each team member take on this role in turn over time.

The Scrum Master typically oversees daily standups.

Some of their duties include:

- Removing obstacles during development

- Ensuring the development environment is set up so that the project can be completed

- Training team members in Scrum and making sure it's being accurately applied

- Maintaining a good relationship between the developers and Product Owner – as well as others outside of the team

- Protecting the development team from external interruptions and distractions

The term "master" isn't used to denote someone who has others working for them. It's used in the sense of "a specialist of a particular subject" in that the Scrum Master should have the best (or at least a very strong) grasp of Scrum compared to others involved in the project. They should be a master of the Scrum framework.

Okay, so we've covered project managers, Product Owners and Scrum Masters – what are the differences between these?

CHAPTER 32:
TITLES

The terms "Scrum Master", "project manager" and "Product Owner" can occasionally be confused. They are each different things.

The Scrum Master is the development team member who coordinates the work of their fellow team members. They ensure that Scrum is understood and applied by all involved.

A Product Owner is the person who has final authority in representing the customer's interests and they interact directly with the client.

A project manager is the individual ultimately responsible for the entirety of a project. There is technically no project manager title in Scrum – those duties are instead shared by the Product Owner and Scrum Master.

Scrum Master is a Scrum term. Product Owner is an Agile term that is also used in Scrum. And project manager is a general term used in many professions and industries.

An impediment is something that blocks or slows progress.

In a literal sense, a tree that falls over and blocks a road is an impediment.

In Scrum, an impediment is anything that prevents the team from meeting their potential. This includes issues that could prevent a project from being completed on time or on budget. It is the Scrum Master's job to handle and remove impediments.

There is a tool in Agile and Scrum to document how much work is left in a project. Let's see what that is.

CHAPTER 33:
BURNDOWN CHART

A burndown chart shows how many hours of work are left on the project day by day during a sprint. The days are displayed left to right at the bottom of the graph and the hours are displayed bottom to top on the left side of the graph.

You can look at the burndown chart to see if the project is on target, running ahead or falling behind.

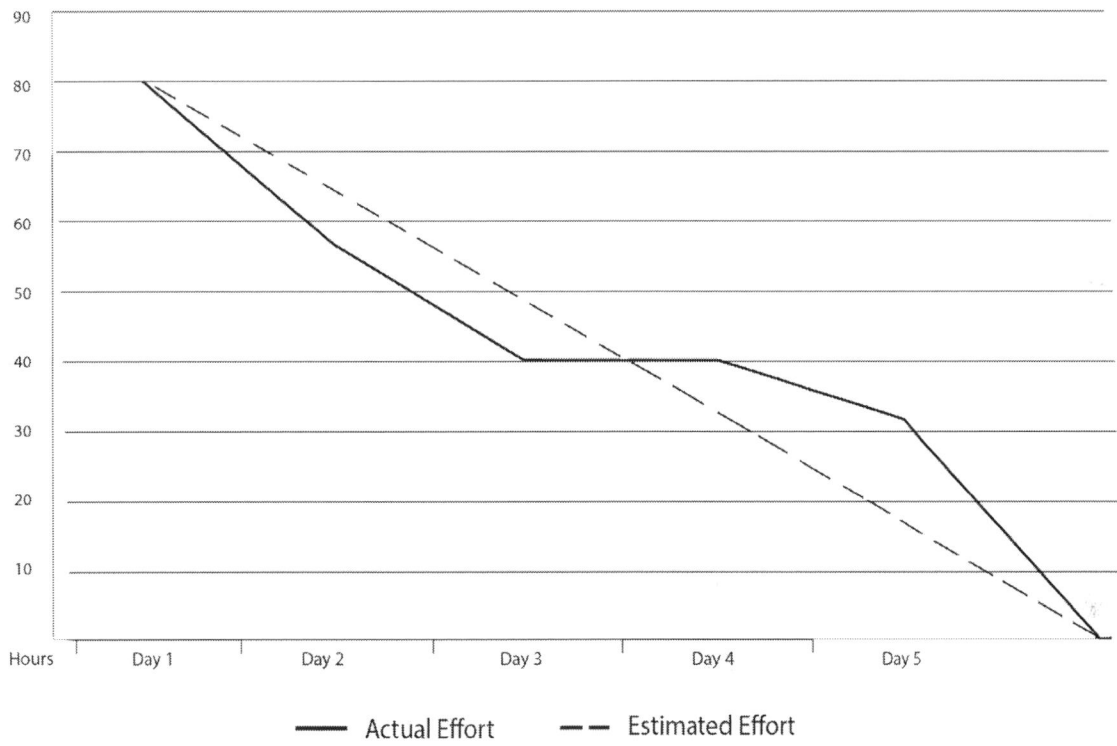

A "product backlog" is the same thing as a backlog: products that need to be gotten; tasks that need to be completed.

A "product backlog item" (also called PBI, backlog item or item) is a single task that is to be completed. It is simply breaking a backlog down into items. PBIs are all the small things that need to happen for production to be completed.

For example, in creating a website composed of ten web pages, each web page could be considered a PBI.

A "sprint backlog" is the task or tasks that a team hopes to complete during a particular sprint.

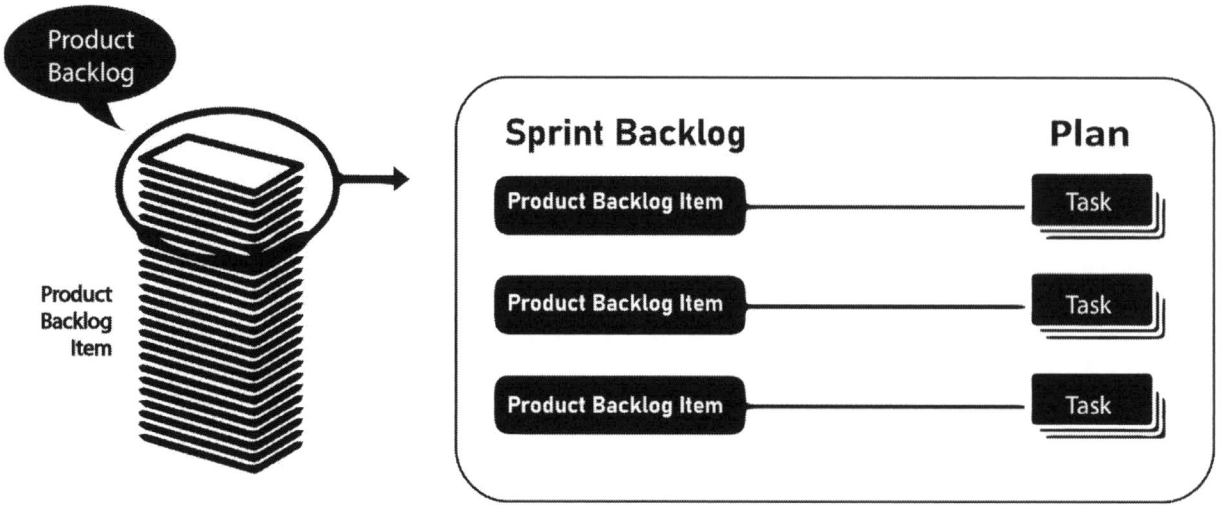

At the start of each sprint, a planning session occurs with the team.

During sprint planning, the sprint backlog is planned out – i.e. the team decides which product backlog items (PBIs) will be completed within the next sprint. Some teams may choose to assign specific tasks to specific developers, but this is not required - many teams decide on the sprint backlog, and let team members choose what task to work on as the sprint proceeds.

A major element of Agile and Scrum is the end users – the people who will actually be *using* the product when it's done. Let's discuss this.

CHAPTER 34:
USER STORIES

A user story is an Agile and Scrum tool that attempts to describe software from the user's perspective.

They are written from the user's viewpoint and are used to document tasks for developers to complete by describing particular features.

User stories include the type of user, what they want, and why.

They are written like: "As a (type of user), I want (some goal) so that (some reason)."

For example, "As a user, I want to log into my account using a username and password so I can access my account information."

Agile and Scrum typically have developers work on tasks in the form of user stories.

In Agile and Scrum, epic refers to a larger body of work (big tasks) that can be broken down into user stories (smaller tasks).

Both epics and stories are examples of Product Backlog Items (PBIs).

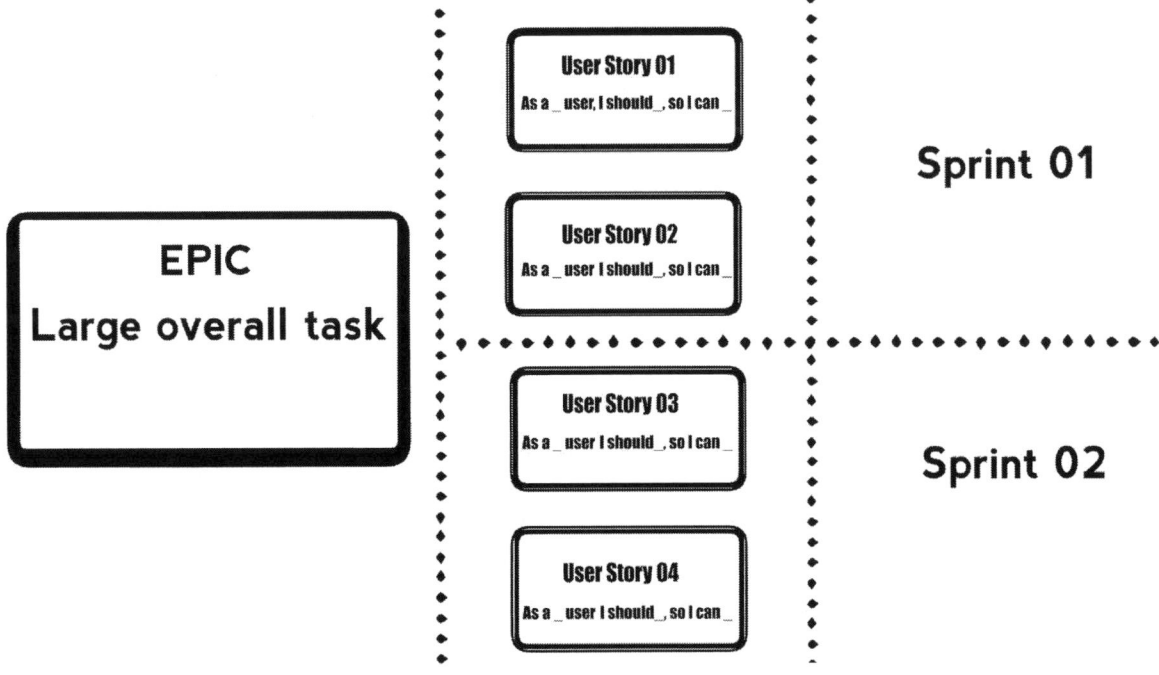

Criteria are the standards against which something is judged – they're the requirements.

Acceptance criteria are the details that provide a clear description of what is considered to be "done" in terms of a user story. For example:

User story: As a user of this website, I want images to expand when I hover the mouse over them so that I am impressed by the interactivity of the site.

Acceptance criteria: All images expand 25% in size when hovered over by a mouse.

A Scrum Board is a physical surface that can be used to visualize information and manage the sprint backlog. This is also referred to as the taskboard.

Scrum Board

In Agile and Scrum, there is a backlog meeting where tasks are gone over. Let's go over this.

CHAPTER 35:
STORY TIME

Story time is a meeting during a sprint when items on the backlog are discussed and clarified. Attempts are made to estimate how long each PBI (Product Backlog Item) will take to complete and tasks are prioritized.

Story time is also referred to as "backlog grooming" or "backlog refinement".

One aspect of this that you should know about is the estimation of task difficulty. There are a number of different methods used in Agile, but the two most common are "T-shirt size" and "Fibonacci sequence". These are methods to indicate how much work is involved in a specific task.

The "T-shirt size" practice involves assigning each task a size of t-shirt that indicates its difficulty. The usual sizes are small, medium, large and extra-large.

The "Fibonacci sequence" practice involves assigning each task a number that indicates its difficulty. These numbers are taken from a popular mathematical sequence of numbers, so named because they were popularized centuries ago by an Italian mathematician named Fibonacci. It is a sequence of numbers where each number is the sum (combined total) of the previous two numbers. It looks like this:

1, 1, 2, 3, 5, 8, 13, etc.

The higher the number assigned, the more difficult the task is.

If a particular task is difficult enough that its t-shirt size or Fibonacci number is outside the ones given above, it often means the task should be examined to see if it can be further broken down into less difficult individual tasks.

Velocity is the speed at which teams complete work. Specifically, it refers to how much of the product backlog can be handled in one sprint.

Once velocity is reliably established over a period of time, it can be used to plan projects and predict completion dates.

Agile and Scrum projects are run through sprints and regular meetings. Let's look at the meeting that takes place at the end of each sprint.

CHAPTER 36:
RETROSPECTIVE

Retrospect means to review or survey past events or a period of time.

A sprint retrospective is the meeting at the end of a sprint where the team determines what could be changed that might make the next sprint more productive. Sprint retrospectives gather feedback and provide info on how a project is progressing.

The meeting can be overseen by the Product Owner (person responsible for defining user stories and prioritizing the backlog), but it need not be – sometimes, this meeting involves only the members of the development team.

Here are some examples of great questions that can be asked during a sprint retrospective:

- What were our successful actions during this sprint?

- What did we learn from this sprint?

- In future sprints, what should we do the same?

- In future sprints, what could we do better?

- Are there any bugs?

- Does anyone have any questions?

- Does anyone have any confusion?

The sprint retrospective usually includes the Product Owner, Scrum Master and the entire development team.

Sprint Retrospective

Meeting after Sprint Review to go over the project

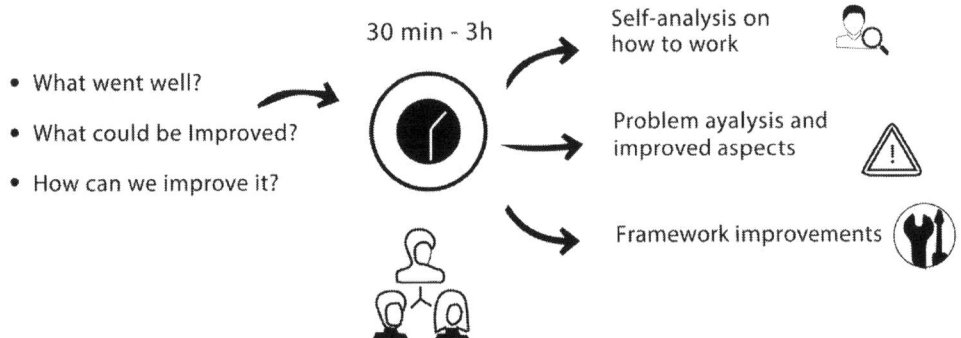

- What went well?
- What could be Improved?
- How can we improve it?

30 min - 3h

Self-analysis on how to work

Problem ayalysis and improved aspects

Framework improvements

Product Owner, Scrum Master and development team

Let's go over the main Scrum roles to clarify each of these further.

CHAPTER 37:
ROLES IN SCRUM

The three main roles in Scrum are:

1. Product Owner.

This person is responsible for laying out the work that needs to be done and prioritizing that work. They are knowledgeable in the project expectations and act as a guide to the team carrying out the project.

Product Owners remain involved with the project throughout its entirety. This is as opposed to a boss who is only involved at the beginning, during initial planning. The Product Owner ensures that the project is adjusted and reprioritized as needed, based on feedback.

With all those duties, the Product Owner does not direct or control the development team's activities – that is handled by the Scrum Master.

2. Scrum Master.

There are two primary duties of a Scrum Master:

1) They protect the development team and make sure that everyone can focus on their work with minimal distractions. This includes isolating and handling impediments that come up.

2) They protect the Scrum process itself and ensure that it is correctly applied. Therefore, the Scrum Master must be knowledgeable in Agile and Scrum. An element of this is acting as a trainer and coach for all other team members.

3. Development team.

These are the individuals that write the code.

The development team includes architects, testers, developers, and designers.

The team acts together to figure out how to achieve their goals. The specific features they work on are based on the priority laid out by the Product Owner.

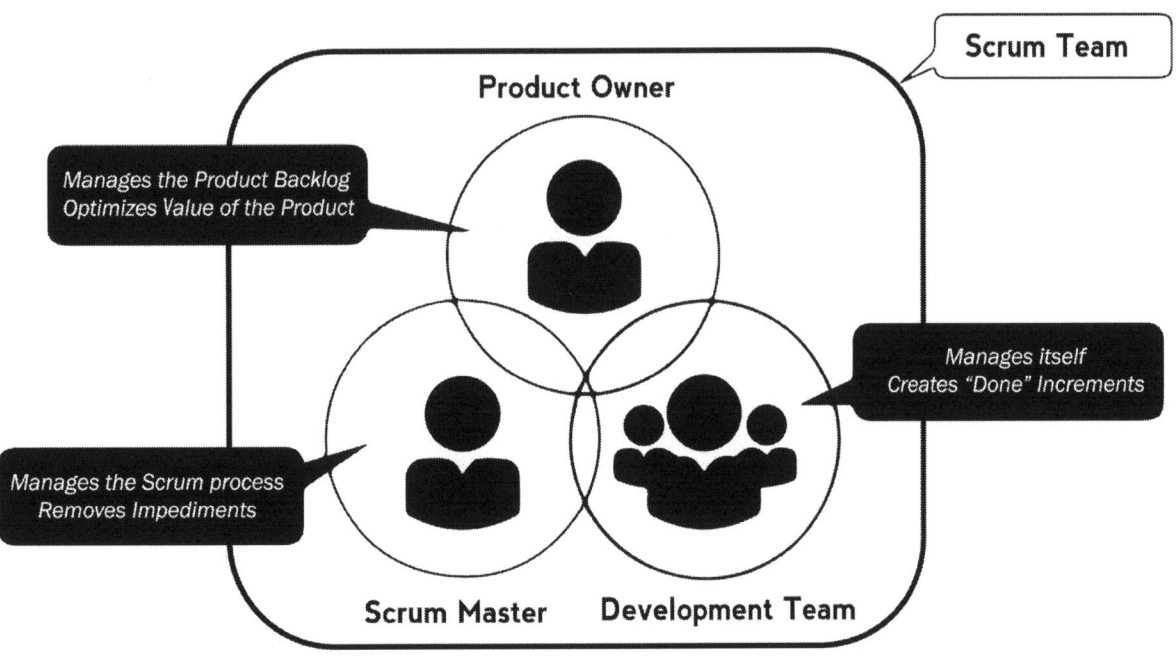

Let's see how all these roles work together on a project.

CHAPTER 38:
SAMPLE AGILE/SCRUM PROJECT

Let's bring Agile and Scrum together by running through an example project.

Let's say Mark has an idea for a new app for his high school basketball fans. Using crowd-sourced (produced by a large number of people) data, parents and friends could get up-to-date scores and standings for any high school basketball team in the country using only their smartphone.

One major problem, Mark doesn't know how to make apps. But Mark does know about Agile.

He gets his friend Samantha, who is a trained developer, to be the Product Owner. Mark is the client. They are both stakeholders.

Samantha creates a product backlog based on Mark's vision and breaks these up into user stories.

Samantha gets a couple of her developer friends to help with coding the app. They conduct daily standups and start each week with a sprint planning meeting. Their daily standups take 15 minutes or less and each person is asked:
- What did you accomplish yesterday?
- What will you accomplish today?
- What obstacles are you facing?

They keep each sprint to 7 days and conclude each week with a sprint retrospective. Each of the members of the dev team are assigned user stories as tasks to complete during sprints. As a note, not all dev teams operate this way - some don't assign tasks at all; instead, they let developers choose what tasks to work on from the sprint backlog as the sprint proceeds.

These sprints force a team to develop under short iteration times to ensure that they remain constantly focused. For example, the end result of an iteration could be a new feature or a large bug fix. Either way, it's something that can be presented to a stakeholder as an accomplishment.

Mark and Samantha meet regularly to go over how the project is coming along.

To help the team coordinate their efforts, they might use the project management application called "Trello". Trello is a collaborative application allowing everyone, Mark, Samantha, and her entire team, to stay in sync across all of their devices and to collaborate from anywhere in the world. This allows real-time coordination affording Samantha's team the ability to meet Mark's product wishes better.

After a few weeks, they deliver an MVP – an app that can be launched in the App Store that will continue to have functionality and features added to it as time goes on.

Let's say Mark finds out that users are barely utilizing the app for basketball scores and standings as originally intended. Instead, he sees that people are mostly ignoring the scores altogether and simply using the application to talk amongst each other via the built-in chat feature. This is not what Mark expected at all but since he is using the Agile methodology, he can quickly change the direction of his app.

Mark holds a meeting with Samantha, where they create a new product backlog list that focuses on enhancing the messaging system. The point is, Agile allows for major shifts and transitions in the middle of the project – it's very fluid.

The Agile software development methodology assumes every project comes with its own special needs and requirements and may need to be adjusted accordingly to complete it. Agile anticipates that the client's needs may change throughout the project and therefore a hardcoded (data that cannot be altered) or planned approach will not suffice; instead, the project will need to adapt quickly to address the evolving requirements.

In Agile, tasks are divided evenly into smaller pieces to deliver specific features for a release. The functional software is expounded upon (added to) in incremental iterations, each adding in new features, with the final product including all the features required by the client. The core principle of the Agile model is that it should be both flexible and adaptable.

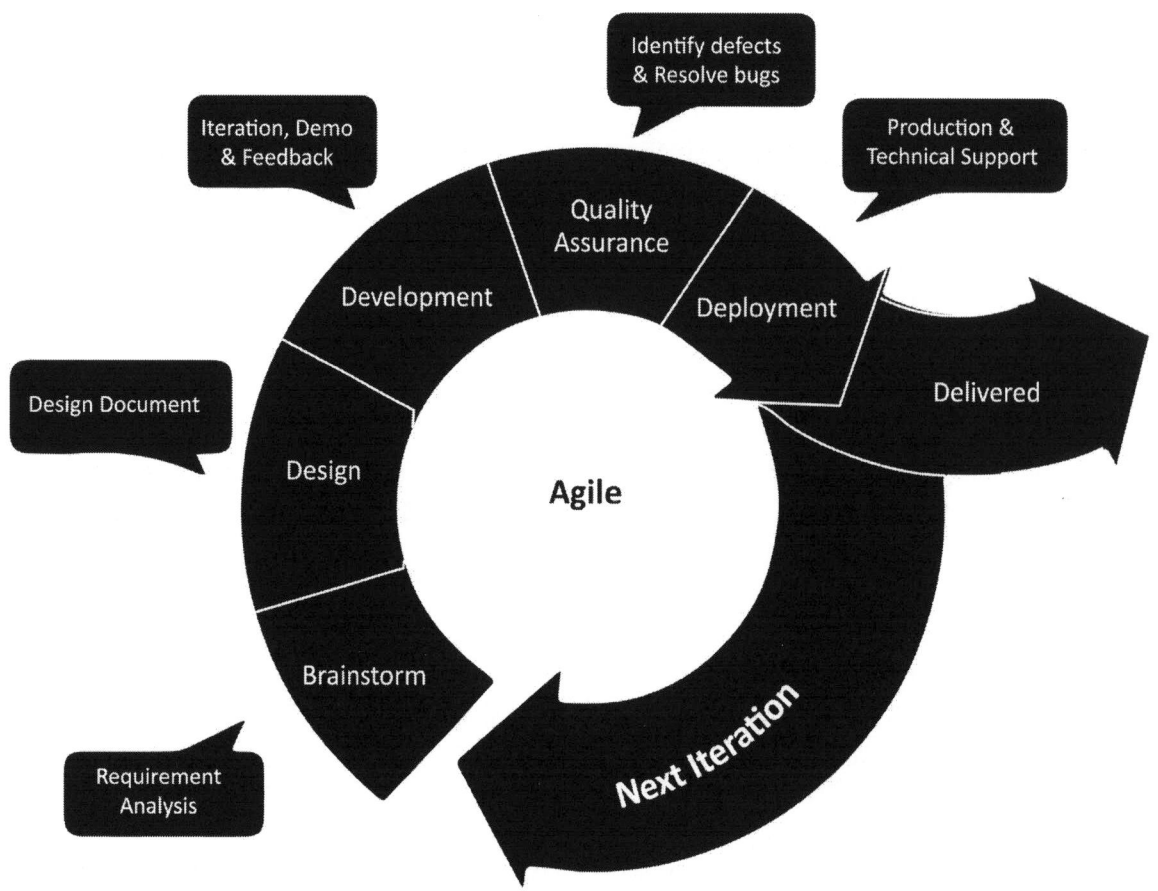

Well done! You now know the fundamentals of Agile and Scrum. With those covered, we will now move into the final project management approach covered in this book: DevOps.

CHAPTER 39:
DEVOPS

DevOps stands for Development and Operations. In technology companies, there are various departments or divisions. Two of these are:

1. Development – the staff that write the code.

2. Information Technology Operations Department (also called I.T. Operations, I.T. Department, Operations Department or just Operations) – the staff that handle information technology operations. Such I.T. operations include: managing the computer systems that hold the actual programs used by the customers, handling emergency situations where there are interruptions in service in the company's computer programs, and handling customer service. The Operations Department also typically oversees the company's computer network, technical support and other non-coding, yet technological, functions.

DevOps is a business practice, rather than a division of the organization; it combines the actions of these two departments and works to establish a high degree of coordination and cooperation throughout a company.

Another element of DevOps is constant testing – referred to as Quality Assurance (QA).

The purpose of DevOps is to speed up the development and improvement of high-quality software.

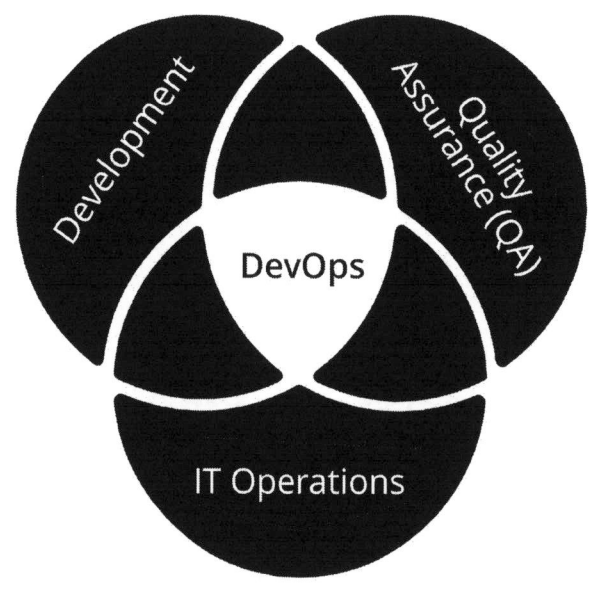

"CI" stands for "Continuous Integration".

Continuous integration is an approach to software development and a set of practices that encourages developers to implement small changes and check-in (upload) code to version control (software for managing different versions of code) repositories (storage) frequently.

This code is collected together in a set of computer files called a "repository". At any point, this code can be converted into an actual computer program that can be run on a computer; that process is called "building" the program, or "creating a build" of the program.

Each time developers merge their code changes into a central repository, CI includes ensuring automated builds and tests are run on the code in the repository.

This is as opposed to not checking in code often or not testing code after every push (an update made to code that is uploaded for review or deployment).

CI is a component of DevOps.

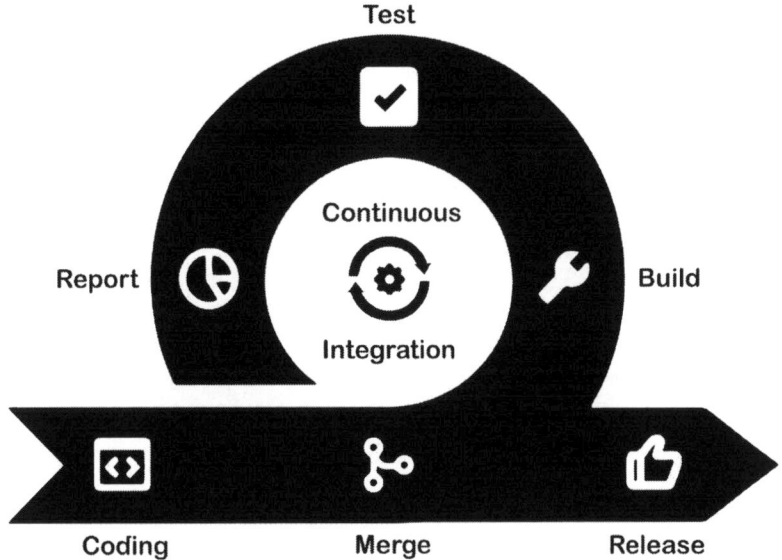

"CD" stands for "continuous delivery". It is another element of DevOps.

CD encourages that development teams produce software in short cycles. CD automates the delivery of applications to environments (a computer system where computer programs are executed and deployed). Since teams sometimes work with multiple environments (such as testing and development), CD ensures that there is an automated way to push code changes to the applicable environment.

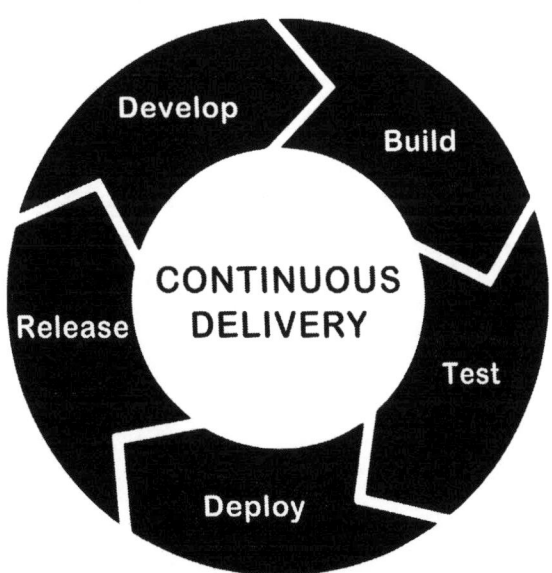

CI and CD include continuous testing to ensure that the end product that is delivered to users has no errors.

CI/CD are commonly used together to refer to the following:

- DevOps is being utilized

- Software is being developed by a team

- Each stage of the process is separated into different environments

- Only small changes are made

- Every change is checked in

- Every step is fully tested before moving forward

There is another approach to software development that we will now cover to enhance your understanding of DevOps.

CHAPTER 40:
LEAN DEVELOPMENT

Lean manufacturing is a methodology that focuses on minimizing waste while maximizing productivity. Some points that are monitored to prevent waste include:

- Overproduction (creating more than is necessary)

- Wasted time (such as waiting)

- Too much inventory (more in stock that what is needed)

- Errors and defects (imperfections; shortcomings)

Lean manufacturing avoids wasted time, actions, motion, supplies, etc. It attempts to achieve as much production as possible through using as little as possible.

This applies to software development. In lean development, one attempts to develop software as efficiently as possible through the same basic principles.

Some of the principles of lean development include:

a. Eliminating waste

b. Enhancing and increasing learning

c. Delivering as quickly as possible

d. Empowering the team

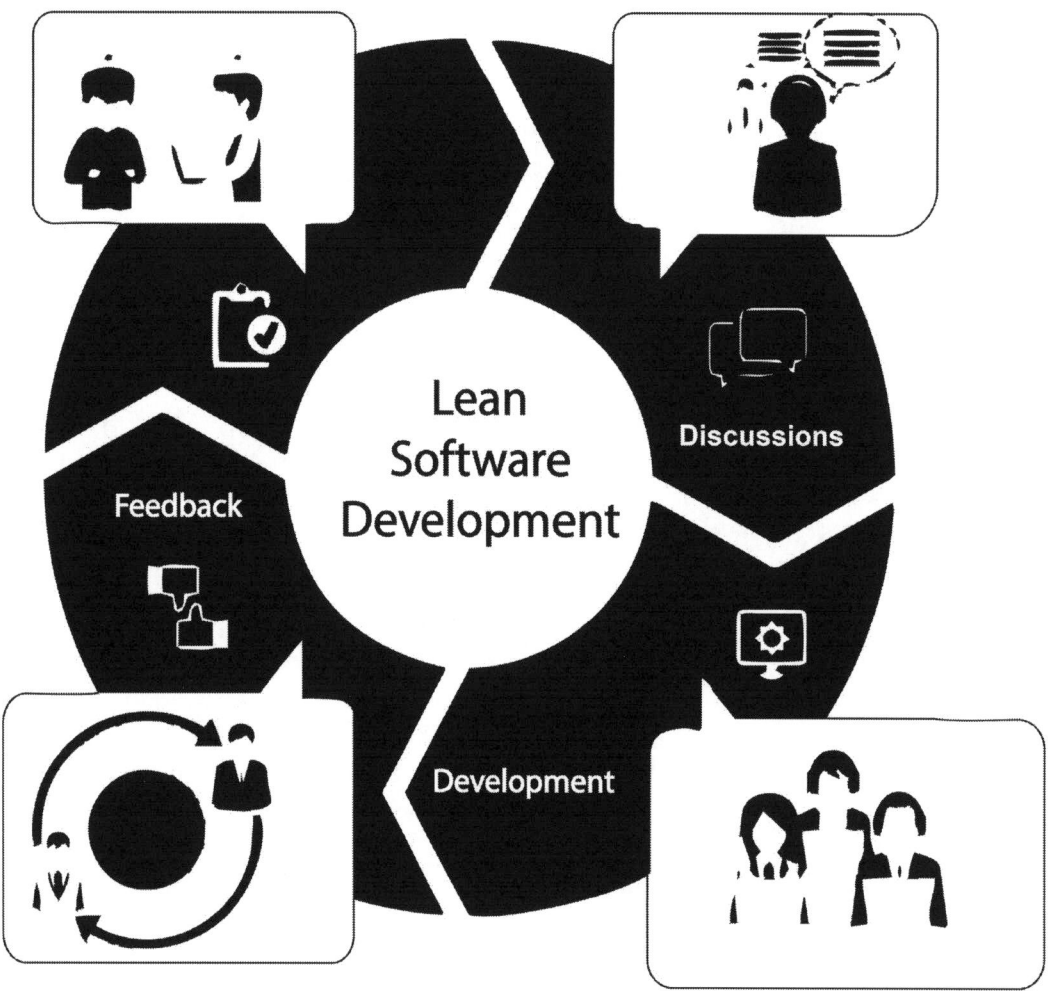

Lean is commonly used in conjunction with Agile because the two subjects mesh well. In fact, sometimes the two terms are used together like Lean-Agile. This simply means that both methodologies are being utilized.

Here's how it relates to DevOps: DevOps represents a change in IT culture focusing on rapid IT delivery through the adoption of Agile-Lean practices. One of the elements of Lean practices is the rapid iterative feedback that you get throughout the entire chain of processes which result in a final product.

In other words, each time something is created, feedback is gathered immediately when something goes wrong (or is about to go wrong) so that you can adjust your operation very rapidly in a very agile manner.

Let's look into DevOps in further detail.

CHAPTER 41:
PURPOSES OF DEVOPS

DevOps focuses on the need for developers and I.T. operations to work closely together to achieve common goals.

Be aware that DevOps is a relatively new discipline and exiting definitions may differ. In general, it's a combination of cultural philosophies, practices, and tools that increase an organization's ability to deliver applications and services at a high velocity. This means evolving and improving products at a faster pace than organizations using traditional software development and infrastructure management processes.

This speed enables organizations to serve their customers better and compete more effectively in the market – specifically, by increasing the velocity at which developers can actually deploy their code, their programs, and being able to improve at a faster pace.

An essential element of DevOps is that there's a change in culture. It's not necessarily about the tools.

DevOps emphasizes *people* and *culture*. It seeks to improve collaboration between operations and development teams. DevOps implementations utilize technology, especially automation tools.

DevOps came into use by capturing the minds of people outside the core development team: people in operations, people in marketing, people in supply and inventory. All these different elements of an organization, they started to look at them like, "Well, wait a minute. What if we all cooperated? What if we all looked at the organization as a whole rather than just from our one point of view?"

An important element of DevOps is *communication* and *collaboration*. A successful DevOps program is a transition in culture that moves away from isolated silos (detached operating environments) and towards a collaborative, cooperative organization. You can get tools that help implement this, but when you get right to it, it's a human process. It involves people being willing to communicate with other elements of the organization. DevOps is all about working with others to really understand their point of view, what's important to them, and getting them to understand what's important to you. It's a genuine collaboration so that at the end of the day, the customer is satisfied.

Another characteristic of DevOps is how various components of development are separated into different environments. Let's look at this.

CHAPTER 42:
ENVIRONMENTS

One thing to examine is the fact that software development involves several different environments.

An environment is a computer system where computer programs are executed and deployed.

An example of an environment is developing and executing a program on a single machine (such as your laptop).

Environments range in size from the single machine just mentioned, to networks of multiple, separate servers (large computers used to store and transmit data). An environment is the overall structure within which a user, computer, or program operates.

In some companies, the following environments are used:

- Development environment – this is where all the coding occurs

- Quality Assurance environment – this is where the code is tested by other developers

- Staging environment – this is where review of the software is done before it is delivered to users

- Production environment – this is the live software that users can access

As you may have guessed, the above environments are actually a sequence that the software moves through. Once a stage is complete, the code is passed along to the next stage. If rejected, it moves back for corrections – if accepted, it moves forward.

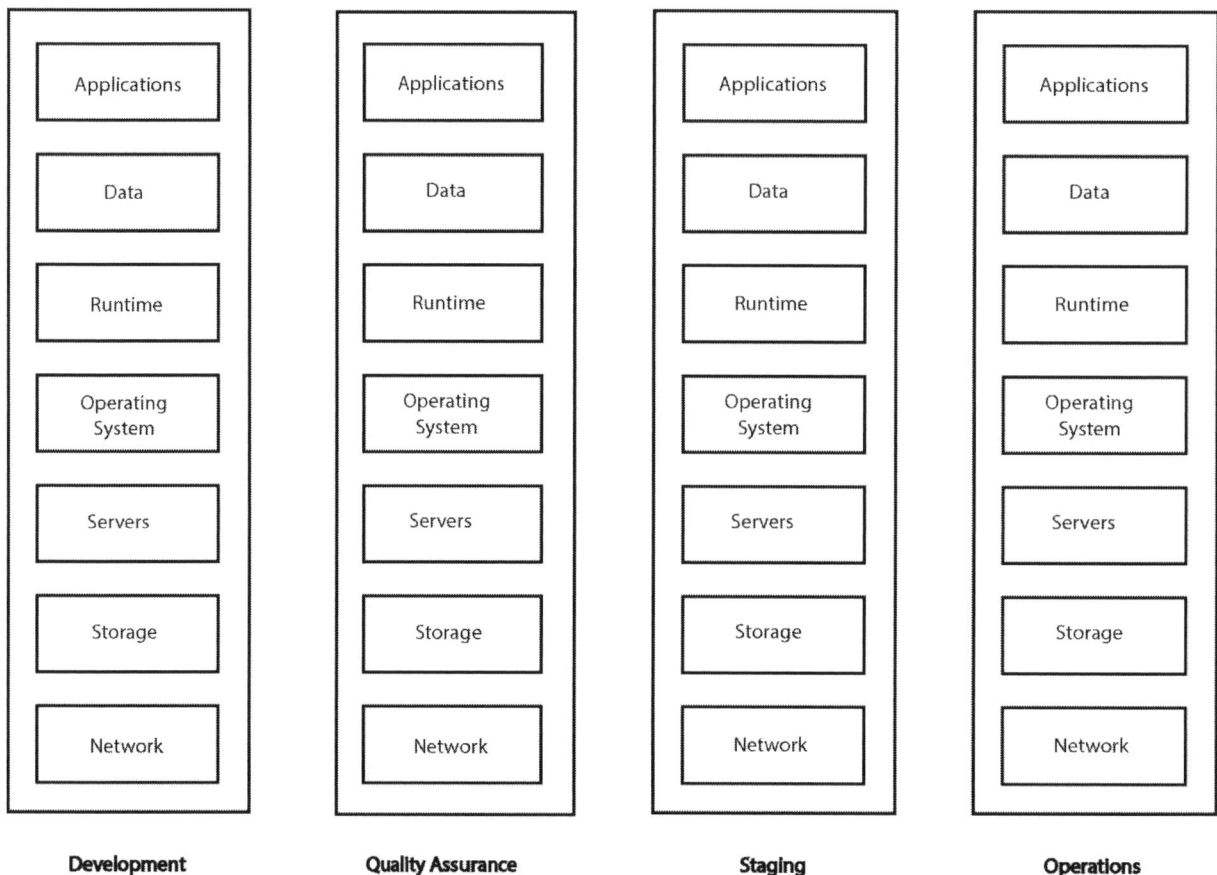

| Development | Quality Assurance | Staging | Operations |

Now, there are a couple of terms in the above picture we need to define. Let's start with runtime.

Run means to start or execute something.

A compiler is a special program that converts the code that looks nearly English, into a form that the computer can understand and operate off of. The product of a compiler would be a set of instructions for the computer to execute that would end up doing what the "nearly English" code described.

Runtime means the time when something in the computer is running. Runtime is exactly what it sounds like – the time when the program is run. You can say something happens at runtime or it happens at compile time.

The term runtime has another, slightly different meaning - one that involves two different types of computer programs. Specifically, it relates to the situation where a custom software program (the kind this whole book is written about) is deployed on a computer for use. Often, that computer program is written in a language that needs some additional help interacting with the core parts of the computer it is on - to do things like access files on the machine, or interact with the various input and output devices attached to the computer, for example. This is accomplished by using another type of computer program that acts as a "bridge" or coordinating element between the computer code in the custom software and the computer code in the operating system on that computer.

That kind of program is called a "runtime library", or "runtime" for short. This program would start up as soon as the computer is turned on and remain running continuously. This way, when technology workers deploy their custom software to that computer, it can actually operate on the computer. One way to think of it is "here is a program that can be used by YOUR program when your program is running."

There are runtime libraries for many of the most popular programming languages used to create modern computer programs. Like most programs, these libraries are usually continuously maintained and upgraded.

An operating system is a special-purpose computer program that supports the computer's basic functions, such as scheduling tasks, running other computer programs, and controlling peripherals (external devices such as keyboards, mice and displays).

Most computer programs will require that an operating system already be installed on a computer before they can function on that computer.

Nearly all computers available today come with an operating system already installed when they are purchased. Computer manufacturers install the operating system before they sell a computer.

Some operating systems are free; others are available for a fee.

One of the most well-known and popular operating systems in the world is called Windows. It is created and sold by the technology company Microsoft.

Other popular operating systems are:

- OS X (created by the technology company Apple – it is used on their desktop computers and laptops)

- Linux (a family of free and for-fee operating systems – it is used on desktop computers and laptops)

- Android (owned by the technology company Google – it is used on mobile devices like smartphones)

- iOS (created by Apple – it is used on their mobile devices like the iPhone and iPad)

A staging environment (stage) is a nearly exact copy of a production environment (the actual code composing a product) for software testing. Staging environments are made to test code and to ensure quality before deploying software. Everything in a staging environment is as close of a replica to the production environment as possible to ensure the software works correctly.

Now that we know those terms, let's look at the diagram again:

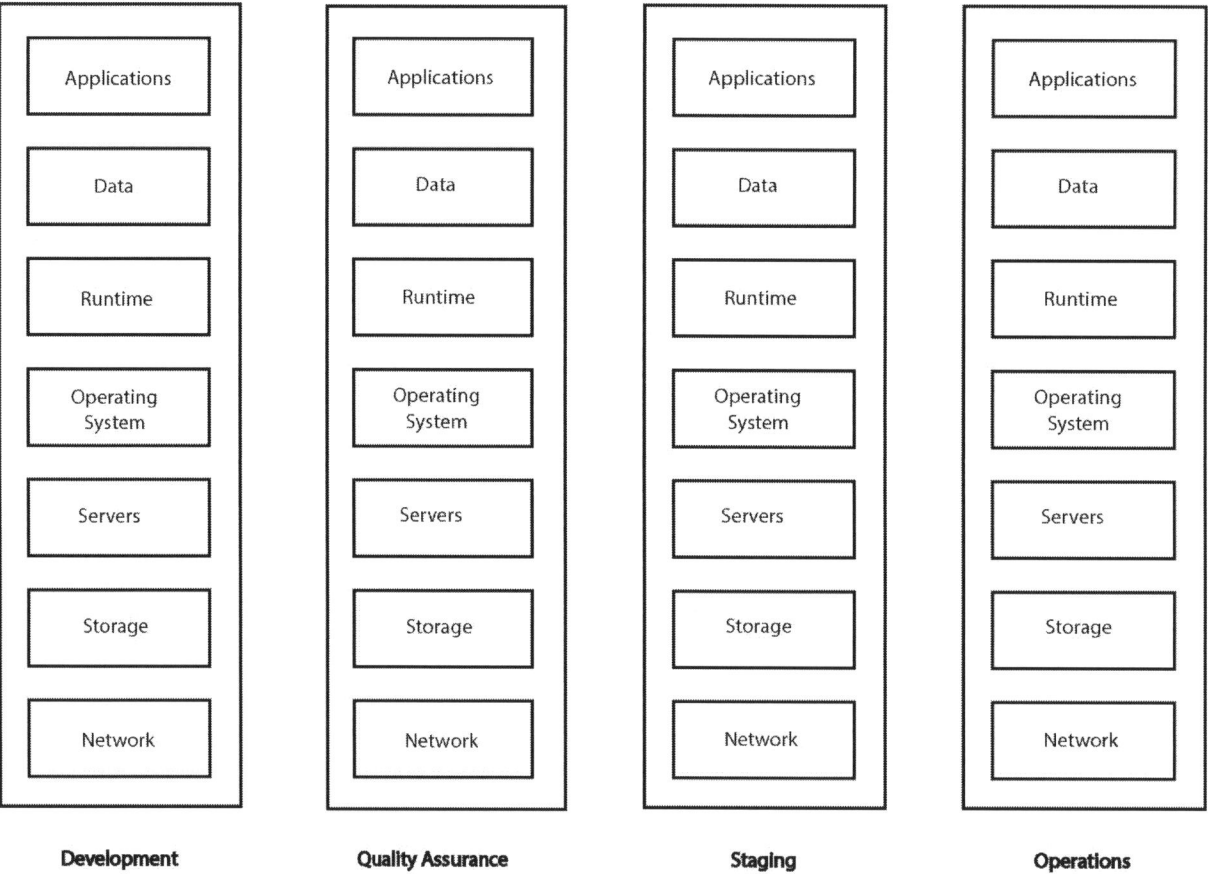

| Development | Quality Assurance | Staging | Operations |

Each of these upright rectangles represents an environment. These environments are kept separate and as chunks of software are completed, they are moved from left to right. Errors are sent back to earlier environments so that fixes can be made. The efficient management of this arrangement, so that viable software is delivered often to satisfied users, is a major aspect of DevOps, and many of the tools you'll find for DevOps relate to how to do this.

Now that you understand the basics of DevOps, let's circle back to project management.

CHAPTER 43:
NOTE ABOUT PROJECT MANAGEMENT

Agile, Scrum and DevOps have exact procedures and rules to them. Yet, you sometimes find that there are differing opinions on how to handle various elements of these tools.

For example, some people believe there are only 4 stages to the project management life cycle, while others feel there are 5.

There are many reasons behind the conflicting data but the primary ones are these:

1. These are relatively new subjects and certain elements are still being figured out.

2. The internet allows anyone to state whatever they want with virtually no regulations. So, authors can publish articles, videos, etc. and say anything – correct or not.

Another thing you may find is that a particular company you work at has a particular flavor of project management they use that doesn't quite follow existing standards and documentation.

For example, you're hired at a company that uses Scrum but they decide that they don't need a Scrum Master. Or the company uses DevOps but doesn't like to test as often as is recommended.

This is simply mentioned here to prepare you for the future.

It is recommended that you follow the procedures and data covered in this handbook.

CHAPTER 44:
PROJECT MANAGEMENT SUMMARY

The four main topics covered in this book were:

1) Project management

2) Agile

3) Scrum

4) DevOps

These are each separate subjects. There are similarities and differences between them all.

Obviously, Agile and Scrum are the most similar — the terms can almost be used interchangeably. In fact, as we mentioned earlier, many of the words used in of Agile are used in Scrum and vice versa.

Project management embraces anything that relates to managing people and getting work done.

DevOps, Agile and Scrum are simply various forms of project management. Meaning, they are ways to manage people and get work done. And as we've covered, Scrum is a subcategory of Agile.

Remember the project management technique covered earlier, waterfall? As a reminder, waterfall is a project management approach where a project is completed in distinct stages and moved step by step toward ultimate release to users. You make a big plan up front and then execute in a linear fashion, hoping there won't be any changes in the plan.

The project management life cycle we covered earlier is a waterfall approach:

1. Initiation (start)
2. Design (plan)
3. Execute (develop)
4. Monitoring (control)
5. Closure (end)

These steps are done in sequence.

As a reminder, the 4th phase is typically done concurrently to the 3rd phase.

It is so hard to predict everything that will occur while developing software. Agile was born in response to this unpredictability.

There are many software products that are in wide use today that don't align with their original vision. You don't always know what users will like or dislike and Agile allows you to respond in real-time.

And as we mentioned earlier, both Agile and DevOps can be used on a project - DevOps as a way to involve multiple sections of a company in the process of designing, creating and deploying software; and Agile as the day-to-day project management style for the development team. Meaning, DevOps involves employees — such as nontechnical people that would not be involved in Agile. For example, in Agile, you wouldn't have your network administrator at a standup.

CHAPTER 45:
CONGRATULATIONS!

Well done on completing our book! You now understand project management and its most popular tech approaches.

We hope you use the data contained in this book to pull off successful development projects that result in high-quality software.

Please look for other Tech Academy books on Amazon and if you're interested in learning to code, check out our coding boot camps.

We also offer custom training classes and other services. To find out more, visit: learncodinganywhere.com.

Made in the USA
Monee, IL
14 February 2020